# GROWING IN TRUTH DISCIPLESHIP

# Growing in Truth Discipleship

## *Week 4: Our Bible, God's Inspired Word*

DANIELIA WILLIAMS-BOSTEDO

*John Yates, Faith Bible Institute*

Blessed with Truth Ministries

# Contents

# Discipleship Day One: What is the Bible? The Nature of Inspiration

*[This is taken from Project One Generation, Faith Bible Institute]*

This week is a reproduction of a discipleship course that I went through, so it has a different layout. John Yates, the writer explains very simply, yet thoroughly, why we can trust our Bible. Days One through Five of Week four of this course are part of the Project One Generation, which is from the Faith Bible Institute. Review Questions are added by me and any text in brackets have been added to the text from the Project One Generation.

The Bible is the basis of everything we believe as Christians. We must have absolute confidence in the truth of the Bible or our faith will crumble. If the Bible is true, we can know with total certainty the nature of God, creation, salvation, morality, the family, eternity and the purpose of life. The Bible is God's revelation of Himself and of His will for us. It is the sole authority for what we believe. However, the Bible is under attack today by those who believe that it is just the word of man. The world is filled with religions, many with their own holy books. How can we know that our Bible and our faith is the true one?

This week, we will examine the Book upon which our faith stands. We begin by looking at what the Bible says about itself. Does the Bible claim to be the Inspired Word of God? What is Inspiration? Let us look to the Bible for the answers to these questions. 2 Timothy 3:16 states that, "*All scripture is given by inspiration of God...*" "Inspiration" here is from the Greek word meaning "God breathed." Simply put, every word of the Bible is straight from the mouth of God. In fact, Matthew 4:4 says it that way: "_______ ____________ *that proceedeth out of the* _______________ *of God.*" Some ask, "But didn't men write the Bible?" Peter answers that the Bible was written down by men who were moved or guided by the Holy Spirit to write the words of God. "*Knowing this first, that no prophesy of the Scripture is of any private interpretation* [no passage was the writer's own personal opinion.] *For the prophesy came* _______________ *in old time by the* _______________ *of* _______________ [man did not decide what would be written *in the Bible]: but holy men of God spake as they were* _______________ *by the Holy Ghost.*" (2 Peter 1:20-21) Any literate person can easily dictate a letter and watch to be certain that every word is correct. Is not an Almighty God capable of insuring that men accurately wrote His words?

Some are willing to accept that parts of the Bible are inspired, but not that **every** statement is absolute truth. The Bible itself declares that the very words, and even the letters are directly from God (Matthew 5:18). Any attack on the Bible is actually an attack on the character of God. If the Bible is God's Word and there is a single statement that is not true within its pages, that would mean that God was either mistaken or lying. God is Truth and cannot lie therefore His Word is absolute truth. He is all knowing and all powerful and therefore can easily reveal, inspire, and preserve His Own perfect Word. You can trust the Bible. It is the world's only perfect book. It is God's blueprint for your life. You and I are wise to make it the foundation of our life and our decisions.

*Review:*

1. What is the basis of everything we believe as Christians, from who God is to key doctrines and the purpose of life? _______________________________

2. What happens if we don't believe it (#1)?

_________________________________________________

3. Does the Bible claim to be the Inspired Word of God? ___________

4. What does "inspired" mean? _______________________________

5. Using 2 Peter 1:20-21, how would you defend the question, "Isn't the Bible written by men?"

_____________________________________________________________

_____________________________________________________________

_____________________________________________________________

_____________________________________________________________

6. Do you trust the Bible? _____________ Why? Or Why not?

_____________________________________________________________

_____________________________________________________________

_____________________________________________________________

*Week Four Memory Verse(s):*

"All scripture is given by inspiration of God, and is profitable for doctrine, for reproof, for correction, for instruction in righteousness:" (2 Timothy 3:16)

*Bible Reading Plan:*

Plan 1: Lesson Scriptures; Proverb of the Day
Plan 2: John 17
Plan 3: John 17; Genesis 40–41
Plan 4: Matthew 7:1-14; Acts 10:1-23; Psalm 17; Genesis 37-38
Plan 5: _______________________________

# Discipleship Day Two: The Prophetic Accuracy of the Bible

*[This is taken from Project One Generation, Faith Bible Institute]*

Today, we begin examining whether there is objective evidence to prove that the Bible is God's Word. Today's test is proposed in Isiah 41:22-23: Only a true message from God can predict the future. How does the Bible stand up to this test? A full **one-fourth** of the Bible was written as predictive prophecy. Over **2,000** fulfilled prophecies are found in the Old Testament alone. If each element of these prophesies which had to be individually fulfilled is counted, there are some **10,000** fulfilled prophesies! How many prophecies have failed? Not one!

Jesus fulfilled **333** prophesies during His earthly life. There are over **100** fulfilled prophesies concerning ancient Babylon. Daniel 11 contains over **100** fulfilled prophesies. The Bible accurately predicted the Babylonian, Greek, and Roman Empires (Daniel 2 and 8). Consider this small sampling of fulfilled prophesies. 1) Israel would spend 400 years in bondage in Egypt and then return to Canaan after God judged their captors (Genesis 15:13-16). 2) Israel would spend 70 years in bondage in Babylon (Jeremiah 25:11; 29:10). 3) Israel would be scattered among the nations, but would return to their land in the last days—fulfilled in **1948** (Deuteronomy 28:25, 64; 30:3; Ezekiel 36:24). 4) The conquests of Alexander the Great and the fact that his Greek Empire would not be passed on to his son, but only divided into four parts at his death (Daniel 8:5-8, 21-22). 5) **Cyrus** of the Medo-Persian Empire is prophesied **by name** over 100 years before his birth as the King who would allow Israel to return to Jerusalem to rebuild the Temple after the Babylonian captivity (Isaiah 44:28). 6) King **Josiah** of Judah is prophesied **by name** (some 350 years before his birth) as the king who would destroy Jeroboam's false altar (1 Kings 13:1-2). 7) Jeremiah predicted (600 BC) the next nine areas of expansion for the city of Jerusalem (Jeremiah 31:38-40). Expansion into the $3^{rd} - 9^{th}$ areas did not take place until the years from 1900 to the 1960s.

To put this into perspective, let us examine a few of the holy books of other religions. The Hindu Vedas have ZERO fulfilled prophecies. The Book of Mormon has ZERO fulfilled prophecies. The Muslim Koran has one self-fulfilling prophecy – Mohammed said he would return to Mecca and he did. Let's review to get a few facts into your memory.

1. _______________ of the Bible was written as predictive prophecy.
2. The Old Testament has _______________ fulfilled prophecies, including some _______________ individual components.
3. Jesus fulfilled _______________ prophecies in His earthly life and ministry.
4. Medo-Persian king prophesied by name 100 years before his birth as king who would allow the Temple rebuilt: _______________.
5. Judean king predicted by name 350 years in advance: _______________.
6. What blows your mind most about the prophetic accuracy of the Bible?

_______________________________________________________________

_______________________________________________________________

Why?

_______________________________________________________________

_______________________________________________________________

7. Does knowing that God predicted so many things in His Word and they came true help you trust the Bible more? _______________
8. What is something that stands out that you could use to help someone who doesn't trust the Bible as truth?

_______________________________________________________________

_______________________________________________________________

_______________________________________________________________

_______________________________________________________________

_______________________________________________________________

*Week Four Memory Verse(s):*

"All _______________ is given by _______________ ___ _______, and is profitable for doctrine, for reproof, for correction, for instruction in righteousness:.." (2 Timothy 3:16)

*Bible Reading Plan:*

Plan 1: Lesson Scriptures; Proverb of the Day
Plan 2: John 18
Plan 3: John 18; Genesis 42–43
Plan 4: Matthew 7:15-29; Acts 10:24-48; Psalm 18:1-24; Genesis 39-40
Plan 5: _______________

# Discipleship Day Three: The Scientific Accuracy of the Bible

*[Taken from Project One Generation, Faith Bible Institute]*

Today we will examine some of the scientific evidences in favor of the inspiration of the Bible. Are there scientific facts stated in Scripture which could not have been known by human authors of the Bible? Let us examine just five of these scientific facts found in the Bible.

1. **The fact that life only comes from life** (Genesis 1:11-12, 21-25). For centuries, it seemed obvious to science that life spontaneously arose from rotting substances, stagnant water, and moist soil. The scientific fact that life only arises from life was not discovered until 1862 and 1865 when Louis Pasteur and Johann Mendel disproved spontaneous generation and proved the laws of genetics respectively.

The Bible declared this fact in its first chapter 34 centuries before man made this discovery. In fact, the theory of evolution is actually still based upon a denial of this fact. Remember, Darwin published his theory of evolution in 1859, before spontaneous generation was disproved and before the laws of genetics were understood.

2. **The fact that the earth is round** "the circle of the earth..." (Isaiah 40:22) The Bible records this scientific fact 22 centuries before man made this discovery. By contrast, the Hindu Vedas state that the earth is flat and triangular.

3. **The fact the earth hangs in space upon nothing** (Job 26:7). God revealed this scientific fact 33 centuries before man made this discovery. By contrast, the Hindu Vedas state that the earth is carried by elephants.

4. **The fact that the stars are innumerable** (Genesis 15:5). This scientific fact was revealed by God 21 centuries before man made this discovery.

5. **The medical facts concerning infection and sanitation.** The Law of Moses laid down extensive, specific and accurate regulations for how to recognize, isolate, and cleanse infection and how to control the diseases spread through unsanitary conditions. These regulations contain none of the ignorant nonsense taught in the 15th century BC colleges of Egypt where Moses was trained and are 30 centuries ahead of man's discoveries.

The Bible not only contains these and many other advanced scientific facts, it also is completely devoid of the scientific nonsense found in other ancient secular and holy books. In the Muslim Scriptures, we read that the sun sets each evening into a muddy pond in the center of the earth (Sura 18:85-86) and that the moon is larger than the sun and shines by its own light. How could the bible avoid all the foolish statements of other ancient books? Because God is the Author!

*Review:*

1. The fact that life only comes from ____________________ can be found in the book of Genesis, declared ________ centuries before man made the discovery.

2. The fact that the earth is ________________ is documented _____ centuries before man made the discovery.

3. ________________ facts concerning infection and sanitation were extensively and actively laid out in the Law of Moses ________ centuries before man's discoveries.

4. Have you ever heard these truths? __________

5. Do these truths help you trust God and His Word? ______________

6. How would you use these Scriptures to help someone who doesn't believe that God's Word is the Word of God?

_______________________________________________________________________

_______________________________________________________________________

_______________________________________________________________________

_______________________________________________________________________

_______________________________________________________________________

7. What surprised you the most about the other "holy" books and what they say about things that we know to be true today?

_______________________________________________________________________

_______________________________________________________________________

_______________________________________________________________________

_______________________________________________________________________

_______________________________________________________________________

*Week Four Memory Verse(s):*

"All ____________________ is given by ______________ ____ ________, and is ______________ for doctrine, for ____________, for correction, for instruction in righteousness:.." (2 Timothy 3:16)

*Bible Reading Plan:*

Plan 1: Lesson Scriptures; Proverb of the Day
Plan 2: John 19
Plan 3: John 19; Genesis 44–45
Plan 4: Matthew 8:1-13; Acts 11:1-18; Psalm 18:25-50; Genesis 41
Plan 5: ____________________

# Discipleship Day Four: The Greatest Book of All Time

*[Taken from Project One Generation, Faith Bible Institute]*

The Bible is the greatest book in the history of the world. It is the number one best seller of all time. Not counting the untold millions of copies which have been printed to be given away, it has outsold the next top five books combined (and four of those five are books about the Bible). It is the first book ever put into codex (modern book) form rather than scroll form. It was the first major book ever translated from one language to another and has been translated into more languages than any other book. It was the first book ever printed. The first act of the congress of the United States was to print Bibles. The Bible has inspired more books than any other book. It contains the oldest written history in existence and was the first book carried into and read from outer space. It is indeed an amazing book, a book authored by God Himself.

The Bible was written over 15 centuries, in three different languages, on three different continents, and by some 40 inspired authors. It was written during times of war and peace, from palaces and prisons, by Jews and Gentiles, by rich and poor, by kings and farmers, and by Jewish rabbis and Christian evangelists. Yet amazingly enough, it is one consistent story from beginning to end—with a supernatural unity that could only be achieved through divine inspiration. Contrary to what some skeptics ignorantly claim, the Bible never contradicts itself and it has unified themes that flow from Genesis through to Revelation.

The Bible has come down to us through a history of sacrifice and blood. In AD 303, after a fierce persecution, Roman Emperor Diocletian erected a column over a burned Bible with the words, "Extinct is the Name of Christian." Ten years later Christianity became the official religion of the Roman Empire. Early translators of the Bible were violently persecuted and put to death. Possessing a Bible is still a crime in many countries. Governments, religions and skeptics have attacked the Bible and yet it stands unshaken. The French skeptic, Voltaire, once declared that the Bible would not exist in another hundred years. After his death, Voltaire's house and printing press were used to print Bibles.

The Bible is the most well attested book of the ancient world, with over 5,600 ancient Greek manuscripts. If all these were lost, we still have almost 20,000 ancient manuscripts in other languages. If all these were lost, we still could duplicate every verse from the 36,000 quotes by the Church Fathers in the first three centuries. If all these were lost, we could still duplicate every verse from the Lectionaries (early

Christian lessons). You can trust that the words of your Bible are the words originally given by God! Let it change you like it has changed the world.

*Review:*

1. Write down some of the things that surprised you most about this lesson.

_______________________________________________________________

_______________________________________________________________

_______________________________________________________________

_______________________________________________________________

_______________________________________________________________

_______________________________________________________________

2. Do you have doubt that the Bible that we have today is the same Bible from the first century or even before that? _______________

3. Why are you sure or why do have doubt?

_______________________________________________________________

_______________________________________________________________

_______________________________________________________________

_______________________________________________________________

_______________________________________________________________

4. Write down either some solid truths that help you trust your Bible or if you have doubts, write some things that you question so that you can talk them over with your mentor.

_______________________________________________________________

_______________________________________________________________

_______________________________________________________________

_______________________________________________________________

_______________________________________________________________

*Week Four Memory Verse(s):*

"All _______________________ is ___________ by _______________ ____ _______,
and ____ _______________ for _______________, for _______________, for correction,
for instruction in _______________:." (2 Timothy 3:16)

*Bible Reading Plan:*

Plan 1: Lesson Scriptures; Proverb of the Day
Plan 2: John 20
Plan 3: John 20; Genesis 46–47
Plan 4: Matthew 8:14-22; Acts 11:19-30; Psalm 19; Genesis 42-43
Plan 5: _______________________

*Put this lesson into action:*

Commit today to spending daily time in the Book that has changed the world.

# Discipleship Day Five: What Translation Should I Use?

[*Taken from Project One Generation, Faith Bible Institute*]

Today, there are over 100 Bible translations in English alone. In many languages, there is only one translation and many languages do not yet have a Bible. For those who speak a language where more than one translation is available, a choice must be made concerning which translation should be used. Sincere Christians with pure motives do advocate various translations. However, all translations are not equal. Here are two key issues to consider when choosing a Bible.

The first issue is the **Translation Method**. Most modern Bibles are translated with the purpose of being as easy to read as possible. This goal sounds good, but accuracy should never be sacrificed for readability. Most modern versions reword or paraphrase the main thoughts of each verse (dynamic equivalency). These Bibles are easy to understand because they are almost commentaries, but this introduces too much danger that the opinions of the translators will be added to the text. The belief that *every word* is inspired leads to the conclusion that we should use a Bible where the *words* themselves are translated as literally as possible (formal equivalency).

The second issue is the **Translation Text**. There are essentially two different versions of the Greek New Testament in existence. The tradition, majority text is based upon thousands of ancient manuscripts from a great variety of geographic areas from many different centuries. This was the accepted text of true Christian Churches throughout the history of Christendom. The newer, critical, minority text is based upon a small handful of manuscripts from limited geographic locations, which were accepted by modern scholars as superior, essentially because they were once believed to be older. This claim to superiority based upon age is no longer accurate now that manuscript discoveries have revealed that both manuscript types undebatably go back to at least the second century.

Since manuscripts of both text types are equally ancient, the wisest course is to trust the Greek Text trusted by Christian Churches for the bulk of Christian history, which was the basis for almost all translations into other languages from the second through the end of the nineteenth centuries.

Modern textual criticism is based upon the theory that the true text of the New Testament was **lost** for over 15 centuries and had to be rediscovered at the end of the 1800s from a small handful of manuscripts of a type that had not been used by Christian Churches since the third century. By contrast, Scripture declares that God will preserve His Word in all generations (Psalm 12:6-7; Matthew 5:18). We therefore recommend Bibles based upon the Traditional, Majority, Received Text.

In the English language, these two principles of Translation Method and Text lead us to recommend the *King James Version.*

*Review:*

1. There is one big difference between the translation methods. Either translations are done believing that ________ __________ is inspired by God and therefore needs to be translated as literally as possible or translations are paraphrased for "readability" and have the danger that the _________________ of the translators will be added to the text.

2. Do you believe that one Bible translation is superior to others? _________ Why or why not?

__________________________________________________________________

__________________________________________________________________

__________________________________________________________________

__________________________________________________________________

3. If you use a Bible other than the King James Version, would you consider comparing your Bible with it to see words and phrases or even complete verses that may have been changed or omitted? _________ This is something to talk over with your mentor who may not use the King James Version. [Using a Bible is better than using **no** Bible!]

---

*Week Four Memory Verse(s):*

"______ ____________________ is _________ by ____________ ____ _______, and ____ ____________ for _____________, for _____________, for ______________, for ______________ in ______________:." (2 Timothy 3:16)

*Bible Reading Plan:*

    Plan 1: Lesson Scriptures; Proverb of the Day
    Plan 2: John 21
    Plan 3: John 21; Genesis 48–49
    Plan 4: Matthew 8:23-34; Acts 12; Psalm 20; Genesis 44-45
    Plan 5: _______________________

*Put this lesson into action:*

Truly consider your Bible. When you are sure that you have the right Bible that you trust, live by every word. (Matthew 4:4)

# Discipleship Day Six: Why You Should Study the Bible

What an amazing gift it is that God left His Word for us! We saw just a glimpse this week of how precious and wonderful the Word of God is. If you recall in Lesson 1.6, we gave an introduction of Bible study. Today, we'll look more at why we should study the bible, as prayerfully this week has opened your eyes to just how much the Bible has changed the world and how much it has the power to change you.

First, we are commanded to study the Word of God. *"Study to shew thyself approved unto God, a workman that needeth not to be ashamed, rightly dividing the word of truth."* (2 Timothy 2:15) To study means to apply the mind to; to read and examine for the purpose of learning and understanding; to consider attentively; to examine closely. Studying is deeper than just reading. It is that meditation that we've talked about previously—thinking about and thinking about, pondering, considering, taking apart and applying it. Why did God command this? So that we can be approved unto Him, not ashamed and know how to correctly discern what is truth.

We are also commanded to live by the Word of God and that it is by the Word of God that we will be judged. *"But he answered and said, It is written, Man shall not live by bread alone, but by every word that proceedeth out of the mouth of God."* (Matthew 4:4) *"He that rejecteth me, and receiveth not my words, hath one that judgeth him: **the word that I have spoken, the same shall judge him in the last day**."* (John 12:48)

While we most certainly should do all of God's commands because they are for our good, let's look at some of that good that should help us realize why we should study the Word of God.

As our memory verse this week tells us, **Scripture is useful for direction in how to live out our daily lives.** *"All scripture is given by inspiration of God, and is profitable for doctrine, for reproof, for correction, for instruction in righteousness:"* (2 Timothy 3:16) All means all and that is all that all means. Scripture is another word for the Word of God. Inspiration means God-breathed. Profitable means useful or beneficial. So, just from the first few words we see that every bit of the Word of God has been God breathed to benefit us. Benefit us how? For doctrine (what is right), for reproof (what is wrong), for correction (how to get right) and instruction in righteousness (how to stay right).

The Bible contains everything available to know God and live to be more like Him. *"**Grace and peace be multiplied** unto you through the knowledge of God, and of Jesus our Lord, According as his divine power hath **given unto us all things that pertain unto life and godliness**, through the knowledge of him that hath called us to glory and virtue:*

*Whereby are given unto us exceeding great and precious promises: **that by these ye might be partakers of the divine nature,** having escaped the corruption that is in the world through lust.*" (2 Peter 1:2-4)

In that one passage, we can see that grace and peace are multiplied; we have all things that pertain to life and godliness and are able to have a part of God's divine nature all through the Word of God. Amen!

**The Word of God reveals direction to our paths.** "*Thy word is a lamp unto my feet, and a light unto my path.*" (Psalm 119:105)

**The Bible also reveals our own hearts.** "*For the word of God is quick, and powerful, and sharper than any twoedged sword, piercing even to the dividing asunder of soul and spirit, and of the joints and marrow, and is **a discerner of the thoughts and intents of the heart.***" (Hebrews 4:12)

Most importantly, **the Word of God reveals the heart of God** as it is God. "*In the beginning was the Word, and the Word was with God, and the Word was God.*" (John 1:1) So, by this revelation of God and His heart, **we are reminded of our purpose in life** (Genesis 1:27; Colossians 1:16). **We are conscious of the penalty for sin** and therefore **aware of souls that are without Him and our duty to share Him with others** (John 3:16-21). **We are motivated to live righteously and holy** so that we can be a good witness to others (1 Peter 1:13-25). **We are reassured of God's love** when we fall short (1 John 1-2; Romans 8:31-39).


*Review:*

1. We are _________________ to study the Word of God. "_________________ to shew thyself approved unto _________, a workman that needeth not to be _________________, _________________ dividing the word of truth." (2 Timothy 2:15)

2. What would you say the difference between reading and studying is?

_______________________________________________________________________

_______________________________________________________________________

_______________________________________________________________________

3. We are also commanded to _______________ by the Word of God and by it is how we will be judged. "He that rejecteth me, and receiveth not my words, hath one that judgeth him: the _________________ that I [Jesus] have spoken, the same shall _________________ him in the last day." (John 12:48)

4. Scripture is useful for direction in how to _____________ out our _______________ lives.

5. Define the underlined words in this verse. "All scripture is given by inspiration of God, and is profitable for doctrine, for reproof, for correction, for instruction in righteousness:" (2 Timothy 3:16)

_______________________________________________________________________

_______________________________________________________________________

_______________________________________________________________________

_______________________________________________________________________


6. 2 Peter 1:2-4 give us blessings that cannot be bought or come from any other place. "________________ and __________________ be multiplied unto you ______________________________________, and of Jesus our Lord, According as his divine power hath given unto us ________ ______________ that pertain unto ________________ and __________________, through the knowledge of him that hath called us to glory and virtue: Whereby are given unto us exceeding great and precious promises: that by these ye might be partakers of the __________________ __________________, having escaped the corruption that is in the world through lust." (2 Peter 1:2-4)


7. The Bible also reveals the __________________ of our path, our own __________________ and the heart of __________________.

*Week Four Memory Verse(s):*

"________ __________________ is __________ ______ __________ ____ ________, ______ ____ ______________ for ______________, for ______________, for ______________, for ______________ in ______________:." (2 ______________ 3:____)


*Bible Reading Plan and Put it in Action:*

Take some time to study the Scriptures in this lesson today. Then Evaluate your Bible reading plan and pick one that you can stick to daily and commit to it.

# Discipleship Day Seven: A Testimony of the Impact of the Word of God

A recent statistic found that only 11% of Americans read their Bibles once a week. This is such a sad statistic when we think about how influential the Word of God is. Many people have heard it over and over again that they need to read their Bibles, but it is still hard for them to choose to make the time. I can only suggest that they have not truly given the Word of God a real effort.

I was saved at eleven but didn't commit to the Lord until I was 32 years old. I was at the end of myself, and God was right there for me. I began to go to church and with that came reading my Bible. It wasn't really mentioned that I should read my Bible. I would just read for the Bible study group that I was in, and I was reading with my kids at home. When I started attending the Reformers Unanimous program, I began to hear about the benefits of being in the Word of God and the program had many weekly challenges that kept us in the Word of God, not just reading the Word but studying and memorizing it as well.

This was life changing for me! How do I know? I had been to the end of myself before. I had even said prayers of "repentance" and my life didn't really change. I had gone to church before and, again, my life didn't really change. Once I started reading, studying, meditating on, and memorizing the Bible, my life began to change. Don't get me wrong. I had to take a step of faith in confessing to God in repentance and walking away from my old life to take repeated steps after Him. I also needed church which kept me grounded and accountable. However, when I talk about a change in me, it was the Word of God that did it! "For the word of God is quick, and powerful, and sharper than any twoedged sword, piercing even to the dividing asunder of soul and spirit, and of the joints and marrow, and is a discerner of the thoughts and intents of the heart." (Hebrews 4:12)

When I committed to the Lord, I was full of hurt and bitterness that showed itself in anger, pride, and violence. I had self-medicated for almost twenty years of my life. I had been tired of my situation. I had been tired of my attitude. I had been tired of my behavior; yet I needed something more. I needed Jesus. I wasn't told how this thing would work. I just started reading my Bible more, studying it, thinking about it, journaling and memorizing it. I enjoyed going to church. I enjoyed learning the new songs, but my home life was still chaotic, and many times I was still reacting in those angry prideful and violent ways until one day I didn't. I had a calm in a time when I would usually explode.

See, there is a renewing and sanctifying work that the Word of God does if we would give it the time and effort. Most people quit before they ever get there. Let that not be you! Give the Word of God your heart. Truly hear these lessons. Learn the verses and explore how they apply to your very life. You will be surprised of the person that is in you! I know I am, and to think He's not even done with me! Hallelujah!

– Danielia Williams-Bostedo

We've all tried to change. We all desire better. None of us are perfect and we want to be better Christians, better spouses, parents, and friends. We want to do better for our society. Yet, we often seek change in all the wrong places and wrong ways. What could it hurt to try the Creator of the universe who knows all and is all powerful? I read a quote once and the writer was talking about how so many Christians go to therapists for help and write off God, the Word of God, and the Holy Spirit. He said, "Scripture is the only reliable manual for soul-study. It is so comprehensive in the diagnosis and treatment of every spiritual matter that, energized by the Holy Spirit in the believer, it leads to making one like Jesus Christ." –John MacArthur.

Don't take my word for it. Don't take his word for it. You can take God's word for it though, and we looked at plenty of things this week which should help you better understand why the Bible is important and reverence it more. "Whoso despiseth the word shall be destroyed: but he that feareth the commandment shall be rewarded." (Proverbs 13:13)

---

*Week Four Memory Verse(s)*

"________ __________________ ____ ___________ _____ ______________ ____

__________, _______ _____ _______________ _______________________, _______ _______________,

______ ________________, _____ ___________________ ____ _________________:." (___

________________ ___:___)


*Bible Reading Plan:*

    Plan 1: Lesson Scriptures; Proverb of the Day
    Plan 2: Philippians 1
    Plan 3: Philippians 1; Genesis 50; Exodus 1
    Plan 4: Matthew 9:1-13; Acts 13:1-25; Psalm 21; Genesis 46-47
    Plan 5: ____________________________


*Put this lesson into action:*

    If you have a testimony of how the Word of God has changed you, write it down and share it with your mentor this week. If not, start today truly letting God have a chance with your heart and for the next four weeks do your best to read, study and meditate on the Word of God daily. If you miss a day, just pick up the next day. The importance is to truly give the Word some effort. At the end of four weeks, write of a testimony of how God's Word has changed you. I guarantee you will have one.